MW00379953

This book belongs to:

____

Made in the USA
Coppell, TX
28 May 2021

56505241R00069